D1171436

mild- America $18.95 Lexile: 800

4/18

POKÉMON DESIGNER

Satoshi Tajiri

PAIGE V. POLINSKY

**Checkerboard
Library**

An Imprint of Abdo Publishing
abdopublishing.com

abdopublishing.com

Published by Abdo Publishing, a division of ABDO, PO Box 398166, Minneapolis, Minnesota 55439. Copyright © 2018 by Abdo Consulting Group, Inc. International copyrights reserved in all countries. No part of this book may be reproduced in any form without written permission from the publisher. Checkerboard Library™ is a trademark and logo of Abdo Publishing.

Printed in the United States of America, North Mankato, Minnesota
062017
092017

THIS BOOK CONTAINS
RECYCLED MATERIALS

Design and Production: Mighty Media, Inc.
Editor: Liz Salzmann
Cover Photographs: Mighty Media, Inc.
Interior Photographs: Alamy, p. 17; AP Images, p. 18; Courtesy of The Strong®, Rochester, New York, pp. 11, 20, 24, 29 (top & bottom); iStockphoto, p. 19; Mighty Media, Inc., pp. 13, 15; Shutterstock, pp. 5, 7, 8, 10, 12, 14, 21, 22, 23, 25, 27, 28, 29 (center); Wikimedia Commons, p. 9

Publisher's Cataloging-in-Publication Data
Names: Polinsky, Paige V., author.
Title: Pokémon designer: Satoshi Tajiri / by Paige V. Polinsky.
Other titles: Satoshi Tajiri
Description: Minneapolis, MN : Abdo Publishing, 2018. | Series: Toy trailblazers | Includes bibliographical references and index.
Identifiers: LCCN 2016962801 | ISBN 9781532110979 (lib. bdg.) | ISBN 9781680788822 (ebook)
Subjects: LCSH: Tajiri, Satoshi, 1965- --Juvenile literature. | Pokémon (Game)--Juvenile literature. | Video games industry--Japan--Biography--Juvenile literature. | Pokémon (Game)--Juvenile literature. | Inventors--Japan--Biography--Juvenile literature.
Classification: DDC 793/092 [B]--dc23
LC record available at http://lccn.loc.gov/2016962801

CONTENTS

Chapter 1

DR. BUG

In 1996, the Nintendo company released a popular new video game called Pokémon. It allowed players to collect and battle monsters. The game became an instant hit. It soon launched a gaming revolution. Pokémon shaped millions of childhoods. Today, it is still wildly popular with gamers of all ages. And it all began with a young bug collector named Satoshi Tajiri.

Satoshi Tajiri was born on August 28, 1965, in Tokyo, Japan. His father was a car salesman and his mother was a homemaker. The Tajiris lived in Machida, a town near Tokyo. As a child, Satoshi spent much of his time hunting bugs in forests near the Tama River. He carefully studied each insect he found. Because of this hobby, Satoshi's friends called him Dr. Bug.

Satoshi also loved television and comics. He watched **anime** and read **manga** comic books. As Satoshi grew older, he stopped hunting insects. Instead, Satoshi began playing **arcade** games.

FUN FACT

Tajiri has said that if he didn't become a game creator, he would have worked in the anime industry.

Satoshi particularly enjoyed catching stag beetles. He would place large rocks under trees. Later, he would lift the rocks to find stag beetles beneath them!

After high school, Satoshi went to college. But he often skipped classes to go to the **arcade**. After college, Satoshi's father tried to get him a job as an electrical repairman. But Satoshi wasn't interested. His parents began to lose hope in his future. They did not know that their son would soon develop one of the most successful video games in history!

Chapter 2

GAME Freak

After college, Tajiri's passion for gaming continued. He spent a lot of time learning new gaming tricks. Today, video gamers can buy manuals and watch videos **online** to improve their gaming skills. But in the early 1980s, gamer resources were limited. Tajiri wanted to read about his favorite **arcade** games. But there were no guides available. So, he decided to write his own. He called it *Game Freak* magazine.

Tajiri handwrote the first issue of *Game Freak*. His friend Ken Sugimori provided the illustrations. Tajiri then photocopied the pages and stapled them together. The first issue of *Game Freak* released in March 1983. It reviewed different arcade games. It also gave readers tips for playing the games.

A bookstore agreed to sell Tajiri's magazine. To Tajiri's surprise, the magazine was a huge success! Tajiri used his earnings to do research for more issues. Later in 1983, Tajiri dedicated an issue to the game *Xevious*. The issue was a massive hit. Tajiri sold 10,000 copies!

FUN FACT

Satoshi's favorite **anime** was *Ultraman*.

With *Game Freak*, Tajiri created a community for gamers. Today, Pokémon fans have a similar community and meet to compete and share their knowledge!

Tajiri had several contributors who helped him produce *Game Freak*. They and Tajiri felt most video games were of low quality. This led Tajiri to another idea. What if he made his own game?

Chapter 3

Zines to SCREENS

Tajiri was not a newcomer to video game development. In his early teens, he taught himself basic **programming**. He even took apart his Nintendo gaming system to learn how it worked!

Tajiri wanted to make a **sequel** to the game Space Invaders. This was a popular game released by Japanese video game company Taito. Tajiri submitted his idea for a sequel to the Sega company's annual Game Idea Awards. Tajiri's idea did not win. The next year, Tajiri submitted another idea to Sega's contest. It was a game called Spring Stranger. This time, Tajiri won the grand prize!

Sega is a famous Japanese video game developer. The company is known for best-selling games such as Sonic the Hedgehog and Phantasy Star.

Tajiri had ideas for other games too. While continuing to produce *Game Freak*, Tajiri started **programming** a game called Quinty. In the game, players flipped floor tiles to defeat their enemies and move to the next level. Tajiri presented Quinty to Namco, a video game company that had inspired him for many years. To his surprise, Namco approved it right away!

Namco released Quinty in 1989 and it was a major success. Tajiri and the *Game Freak* magazine team were now a game developing company. Tajiri decided to continue using the name Game Freak for the company. Meanwhile, Tajiri was already thinking about his next big project.

FUN FACT

In the United States, Quinty was renamed Mendel Palace.

Chapter 4

The Waiting GAME

ajiri's next idea was inspired by Nintendo's Game Link Cable. The Nintendo Company created this cable for its handheld gaming device, Game Boy. Two players could connect their Game Boys with the cable. This let them compete with one another. But Tajiri saw the cable could also be a tool for communication. He imagined insects traveling across the cable. This vision led to Pokémon.

Tajiri dreamed of a game where players could collect objects. He wanted gamers to know the

The Game Boy product line has sold over 200 million units worldwide!

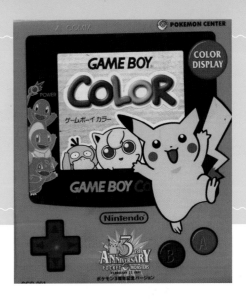

Game Boy screens had greenish-gray or black-and-white displays until Game Boy Color came out in October 1998.

excitement he felt while collecting bugs. However, Tajiri knew that bugs would not appeal to everyone. Instead, he created imaginary monsters for players to collect. He called these creatures Pokémon.

Tajiri knew that Nintendo was looking for a new game. So, he showed his idea to the company. The Nintendo representatives liked the game. But they thought it would take too long to make. They needed to release a new game right away. So, Nintendo offered Tajiri a chance to create a different game that would be faster to create than Pokémon. In response, Game Freak developed the puzzle game Yoshi.

Nintendo released Yoshi in 1991. The game was very popular. The success of Yoshi proved that Tajiri was a talented video game designer. So, Nintendo agreed to release Pokémon once it was finished.

Chapter 5

POKY *Progress*

ajiri and Game Freak worked hard on the Pokémon game. They knew Pokémon wouldn't be much fun if there were only a few monsters to trade. So, the team decided to create 150 different monsters for the game. Then, Shigeru Miyamoto offered a suggestion. Miyamoto was a designer for Nintendo and an important **mentor** to Tajiri.

Miyamoto's idea was to release two **versions** of the game. The 150 Pokémon would be divided between the two games. This way, players would have to trade with friends to collect all of the Pokémon! So, one version of the game was named Pokémon Red. The other was Pokémon Green.

Pokémon's most well-known monster is Pikachu. There has been a Pikachu balloon in every Macy's Thanksgiving Day parade since 2001.

It took six years to create the two games. During this time, Game Freak started to run out of money. Tajiri was unable to pay his employees their full wages. Despite the challenges, the team didn't give up. On February 27, 1996, Nintendo released Pokémon Red and Pokémon Green in Japan.

The games were a hit! A clever **marketing** plan helped raise the Pokémon games' popularity. Just before the release of Pokémon Red and Pokémon Green, the Game Freak team had added an extra, secret Pokémon. This 151st Pokémon was named Mew. Mew was much harder to find than the other Pokémon. Soon, players became **obsessed** with this mysterious Pokémon.

Chapter 6

Fame in the CARDS

The Pokémon games continued to sell well. Players enjoyed collecting and trading with one another, just as Tajiri thought they would. And they were excited about Mew. But Nintendo knew it had to offer something new to keep players interested.

Nintendo worked with **manga** publisher Media Factory to create a Pokémon trading card game. The card game came out in October 1996. It featured the same Pokémon that were in the video games.

The Pokémon Trading Card Game was an instant success. It offered gamers a whole new way to enjoy Pokémon. They could still battle each other and trade with their friends, just like in the video games. But now they could have a physical collection of Pokémon as well!

Card Anatomy

NAME

HP OR HIT POINTS

IMAGE

POKÉ POWER

ENERGIES NEEDED

WEAKNESS

MOVE NAME

PICTURE ILLUSTRATOR

CARD NUMBER

BASIC **Squirtle** HP 60

NO. 007 Tiny Turtle Pokémon HT: 1'08" WT: 19.8 lbs.

Ability **Shell Shield**

As long as this Pokémon is on your Bench, prevent all damage done to this Pokémon by attacks (both yours and your opponent's).

Water Splash 10+

Flip a coin. If heads, this attack does 20 more damage.

weakness   resistance

×2

retreat

It shelters itself in its shell then strikes back with spouts of water at every opportunity.

©2012 Pokémon   Illus. Kanako Eo   29/149

Chapter 7

MONSTER *Smash*

The Pokémon Trading Card Game brought Pokémon to a whole new medium. Its success lead Nintendo to try another printed Pokémon companion. The company worked with publishing company Shogakukan. Shogakukan created a **manga** comic book series based on the Pokémon games. It was called *Pocket Monsters Special*.

The first *Pocket Monsters Special* volume came out in March 1997. The manga featured a main character on a quest to collect all of the Pokémon. Tajiri was extremely pleased with the comic. It perfectly captured the world that Tajiri had spent years building. Meanwhile, Nintendo was also working on a *Pokémon* **anime** television series. It first aired in April 1997. *Pokémon* soon became the most popular children's show in Japan.

By 1998, Nintendo was ready to bring the Pokémon brand to the United States. The *Pokémon* TV series was first broadcast in the

FUN FACT

The main character in the Japanese manga and anime was named Satoshi. He was named after Satoshi Tajiri.

Ash Ketchum is the main character's name in the US versions of Pokémon. Pikachu is his sidekick.

United States on September 5, 1998. A few weeks later, the Pokémon video games Pokémon Red and Pokémon Blue were released. The TV show and the new games were very popular in the United States. It was clear that Pokémon's success was not limited to Japan.

Chapter 8

MARKETING
Masterminds

Tajiri's creation was a sensation in the United States. The success of the TV series created more and more interest in the games. Nintendo wasted no time **marketing** to fans. Soon, there was a Pokémon product for every occasion. Children could start their mornings with Pokémon brand **waffles**, and then carry Pokémon brand backpacks to school. But not before brushing their teeth with Pokémon brand toothbrushes, of course!

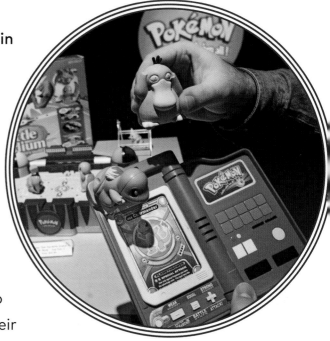

Pokémon toys were so popular that they were featured at the 2000 American International Toy Fair.

In the Pokémon Trading Card Game, Energy cards are used to strengthen Pokémon during battles.

The Pokémon market was exploding. But Nintendo was concerned that interest would fade. It had seen this happen to other toy trends, such as Beanie Babies. So, in 1998, Nintendo and Game Freak formed the Pokémon Company. This company would manage the Pokémon brand.

The Pokémon Company **marketed** its products carefully. First, the company stayed true to Pokémon's basic story and themes. Second, it avoided marketing products to very young children. This helped keep the brand popular with older children. Finally, it chose specific Pokémon for different products. This thought and care kept the brand alive.

In December 1998, the Pokémon Trading Card Game was released in the United States. Nintendo carefully chose the number of characters to include. The company didn't want it to be too easy or too hard for people to collect them all. This new game increased the popularity of Pokémon in the United States even more.

Chapter 9

Pokémon FLU

The many new Pokémon products kept the Pokémon Company very busy. But the video game world was not forgotten. Nintendo began releasing Pokémon **spin-off** games. These games gave fans fun new ways to enjoy the Pokémon universe.

In June 1999, Pokémon **Pinball** was released for the Game Boy Color. The same month, Nintendo released Pokémon Snap for the Nintendo 64 game system. This game featured exciting **3-D** images. Then, on October 19, 1999, Pokémon Yellow was released in the United States.

With the cards and new games, Pokémon was hotter than ever. And Nintendo used this timing to its advantage. It worked with film company Warner Brothers to create a Pokémon movie. *Pokémon: The First Movie* was released on November 10, 1999.

There is an entire store just for Pokémon products at the Kansai International Airport in Japan!

The movie was a huge hit with child fans. Many parents enjoyed the film too. But schoolteachers were not as thrilled. November 10 was a school day and many children skipped school to see the film. News reports said these absences were caused by the "Pokémon flu."

Chapter 10

MONSTER *Makers*

Game Freak and Nintendo continued to develop new Pokémon games. On October 14, 2000, Nintendo released Pokémon Gold and Silver for the Game Boy Color. These new games had the same themes, goals, and Pokémon of the first four games. But Gold and Silver also introduced 100 brand-new Pokémon!

1 A Game Freak designer draws a new Pokémon. The designer fills in the Pokémon's outline to create a black **silhouette**.

2 The silhouette is carefully compared to all existing Pokémon. If it looks too similar to a current monster, it is rejected. If it is different enough, it moves to the next step!

3 The new Pokémon's color scheme is compared to all existing Pokémon. If it is too similar to any existing Pokémon, it is changed.

4 When the Pokémon is finished, the designer presents it to a team of Game Freak employees.

5 If the team approves the design, the Pokémon is then presented to the art director. If the art director approves the new Pokémon, it is included in the game.

Chapter 11

Ready, Set, GO!

Between the video games, cards, comics, TV show, and movies, the Pokémon brand seemed to be everywhere. But there were no Pokémon apps for **smartphones** and **tablets**. Then, in 2014, the Pokémon Company let Google Maps feature Pokémon in an April Fool's Day promotion.

Google Maps is a popular digital mapping service used on smartphones and tablets. In the promotion, people could use Google Maps to find Pokémon in their area on April Fool's Day. This promotion inspired a Pokémon app.

FUN FACT

Pokémon GO has broken five Guinness World Records. This includes fastest mobile game to earn $100 million.

The app was created by Niantic Labs. Niantic's founder, John Hanke, wanted to make a location-based game for **mobile** devices. He saw the Google Maps promotion. Hanke realized that using Pokémon in his game would create a big hit. Nintendo said Hanke could develop the game. The result was an app called Pokémon GO.

Pokémon GO is popular with people of all ages around the world. All you need is a smartphone or tablet and you're ready to go!

Pokémon GO was released in the United States in July 2016. The app allowed players to collect, train, and battle Pokémon right from their **smartphones** and **tablets**. But to find Pokémon, they had to walk around. Different Pokémon would appear on their screens as they arrived in different physical locations in the real world. After one week, Pokémon GO became the United States' most popular **mobile** game of all time!

Chapter 12

Poké-NOW

Sometimes, a game becomes more than a game. Satoshi Tajiri wanted to make kids' lives better. Through Pokémon, he hoped to give players the same sense of wonder that he felt as a child collecting bugs. With Pokémon GO, Tajiri's dream came to life. Gamers experienced the thrill of collecting adventures in the real world.

And Game Freak continues to develop new Pokémon games. In November 2016, Nintendo released Pokémon Sun and

Collectors can buy special boxes for storing their Pokémon cards.

Some rare Pokémon trading cards are valued at thousands of dollars!
But they remain a popular game for kids to play too.

Pokémon Moon. These newest games introduced even more Pokémon. There are currently 802 different monsters for players to catch.

The Pokémon brand is a video game legend. With the help of clever **marketing**, it became a worldwide **phenomenon**. Over the past twenty years, the joy of collecting, battling, and trading has not faded. Only time will tell what is next for the hundreds of Pokémon. But it is certain that gamers will keep working to catch them all!

TIMELINE

1965

Satoshi Tajiri is born in Tokyo, Japan, on August 28.

1989

Tajiri's first video game, Quinty, is released by Namco.

1996

Pokémon Red and Green are released on February 27. The Pokémon Trading Card Game is released in October.

1983

Tajiri publishes his first issue of *Game Freak*.

1991

Nintendo releases Game Freak's puzzle game Yoshi.

1997

The first *Pocket Monsters Special* manga is published in March. The Pokémon anime television series first airs in April.

Pikachu was chosen to be Ash´s sidekick because he was popular with both boys and girls.

1998

The Pokémon TV series, Pokémon video games, and Pokémon Trading Card Game are released in the United States. Nintendo forms the Pokémon Company.

2000

Pokémon Gold and Silver are released in October.

1999

Pokémon Yellow is released in the United States in October. *Pokémon: The First Movie* opens in the United States on November 10.

2016

Pokémon GO is released in July. It becomes the most popular mobile game in the United States.

Glossary

anime – a style of animation that originated in Japan.

arcade – an amusement center that has coin-operated games.

manga – a Japanese comic book or graphic novel.

marketing – the activities done to make buyers aware of and want to buy a service or product.

mentor – a trusted adviser or guide.

mobile – capable of moving or being moved.

obsessed – able to think of nothing else.

online – connected to the Internet.

phenomenon (fih-NAH-muh-nahn) – a fact or event that is rare or extraordinary.

pinball – a game in which a metal ball rolls around a slanted surface and bounces off obstacles.

program – to write computer software.

sequel (SEE-kwuhl) – a book, movie, or other work that continues the story begun in a preceding one.

silhouette (sih-luh-WEHT) – a dark outline seen against a lighter background.

smartphone – a cell phone that can connect to the Internet.

spin-off – something that imitates or comes from an earlier work or product.

tablet – a flat, rectangular mobile computing device with a touch screen.

three-dimensional (3-D) – having three dimensions, such as length, width, and height. Something that is three-dimensional appears to have depth.

version – a different form or type of an original.

waffle – a flat, round breakfast cake with an indented grid pattern.